G000066522

AQUARIUS

This Book Belongs To

_____

AQUARIUS

The Sign of the Water Bearer
January 21 — February 19

By Teresa Celsi
and Michael Yawney

Ariel Books

Andrews and McMeel
Kansas City

AQUARIUS

ISBN: 0–8362–3069–8
Library of Congress Catalog Card Number: 93–73363

Contents

Astrology

An Introduction

Early in our history, as humankind changed from hunter-gatherers to farmers, they left the forests and moved to the plains, where they could raise plants and livestock. While they guarded their animals at night, the herders gazed up at the sky. They watched the stars circle Earth, counted the days between moons, and perceived an order in the universe.

Astrology was born as a way of finding a meaningful relationship between the movements of the heavens and the events on Earth. Astrologers believe that the celestial dance of planets affects our personalities and destinies. In order to better understand these forces, an astrologer creates a chart, which is like a snapshot of the heavens at the time of your birth. Each planet—Mercury, Venus, Mars, Jupiter, Saturn, Uranus, Neptune, and Pluto—has influence on you. So does the place of your birth.

The most important element in a chart is your sun sign, commonly known as your astrological sign. There are twelve signs of the zodiac, a belt of sky encircling Earth that is divided into twelve zones. Whichever zone the sun was in at your time of birth determines your sun sign. Your sun sign influences conscious behavior. Your moon sign influences unconscious behavior. (This book deals only with sun signs. To find your moon sign, you must look in a reference book or consult an astrologer.)

Each sign is categorized under one of the four elements: *fire*, *earth*, *air*, or *water*. Fire signs (Aries, Leo, and Sagittarius) are creative and somewhat self-centered. Earth signs (Taurus, Virgo, and Capricorn) are steady and desire material things. Air signs (Gemini, Libra, and Aquarius) are clever and intellectual.

Water signs (Cancer, Scorpio, and Pisces) are emotional and empathetic.

Each sign has one of three qualities—*cardinal, fixed,* or *mutable*—which shows how it operates. Cardinal signs (Aries, Cancer, Libra, and Capricorn) use their energy to lead in a direct, forceful way. Fixed signs (Taurus, Leo, Scorpio, and Aquarius) harness energy and use it to organize and consolidate. Mutable signs (Gemini, Virgo, Sagittarius, and Pisces) use energy to transform and change.

Every sign has a different combination of an element and a quality. When the positions of all the twelve planets are added to a chart, you can begin to appreciate the complexity of each individual. Astrology does not simplify people by shoving them into twelve personality boxes; rather, the details of your chart will be amazingly complex, inspiring the same awe those early herders must have felt while gazing up into the mystery of the heavens.

The Sign of the Water Bearer

T he symbol for Aquarius, a Water Bearer pouring from a large jug, reveals much about this sign. Rather than touch or drink the water, which symbolizes emotion in astrology, the Water Bearer brings the liquid of life to others. Aquarius is able to bring sustenance to humankind because it remains emotionally detached.

Ruled by the planet Uranus, which

was discovered around the time of the American and French revolutions, Aquarius embodies many of the ideals of equality, freedom, and democracy that marked those years. The Water Bearer loves a cause—especially one that promises to make the world a better place.

Uranus was the first planet to be discovered with a telescope, so it's no surprise that Aquarius has an affinity for high technology. However, the socially conscious Water Bearer will most likely search for ways in which high technology can be used to benefit Earth and everyone living on it.

Character and Personality

Its contradictions and complexities make the Aquarian fascinating. Here is an oddball who loves people, a reformer who keeps its personal life off-limits, a genius who can't remember the date.

The actor who became president (Ronald Reagan) and the wise man who presided over the nation during the Civil War (Abraham Lincoln) were both complex Water Bearers who let nothing keep them from their goals.

Aquarius is a fixed (focused) air (mental) sign who is sincerely convinced its ideas are "right." Whether it's a political, social, or family issue, the Water Bearer easily sees the big picture and works effectively at problem solving or helping others help themselves.

Aquarians are great talkers who are energized by exchanging ideas. Talk show host Oprah Winfrey is a perfect example of an Aquarius who relates well to all people, regardless of race, sex, or nationality. The Water Bearer transcends boundaries and seeks common ground.

Having many kinds of friends and circulating in different social circles is one way Aquarius maintains a wide perspective. Aquarius understands groups, masses, and even mobs much better than it does any one individual.

The Water Bearer treats everyone equally: Friends, strangers, and enemies all receive the same courteous attention. To those who would like to get closer, this behavior may seem cool. However, Aquarius's sincere interest in what makes others tick draws people to it like a magnet.

This sign is in love with the future. Aquarius sees possibilities that may seem outrageous to others. Who could conceive of an electric light, imagine we evolved from apes, or find a way out of the Great Depression? Thomas Alva Edison, Charles Darwin, and Franklin Delano Roosevelt changed our lives because their unbending Aquarius principles let nothing dim their hopes for success.

This focus on the future can cause some difficulty in the present, however. The typical Water Bearer forgets things—names, phone numbers, appointments. Where are those receipts? Such mundane matters are a real challenge for the forward-looking Aquarius.

Signs and Symbols

Each sign in the zodiac is ruled by a different planet. Aquarius is ruled by Uranus and symbolized by a Water Bearer who carries life-giving liquid to everyone.

Aquarius combines the air element of intelligence with the fixed quality of harnessed energy and has free-thinking, humanitarian tendencies.

The eleventh sign of the zodiac, Aquarius is essentially friendly, innovative, un-predictable, and eccentric. Twenty-two is its lucky number.

The day of the week associated with Aquarius is Saturday. This sign rules the shins and ankles. Pure white, electric blue, and psychedelic hues are Aquarian colors. Swans and other large migratory birds are associated with this sign. Its gemstone is amethyst, and its metal is aluminum. White lilacs and orchids are Aquarius's plants, and dried fruits and frozen edibles are the foods associated with this sign.

Health and Fitness

An air sign, Aquarius approaches health and fitness intellectually. This sign is especially aware of how one's mental health can affect one's physical well-being. Healing the body using mental techniques such as biofeedback, mind control, and meditation can be very effective for this sign. Aquarius rules faith healers, and many Water Bearers are open to those with unconventional approaches to wellness.

Air signs are especially vulnerable to airborne allergies, such as hay fever and viruses. A home air purifier could help many Water Bearers who are particularly sensitive to pollen and pollution.

Since Aquarius rules the ankles and shins, exercises that strengthen these areas are important. This sign also rules the circulation, so regular exercise is also necessary. Easy-going aerobics and group jogging appeal to the gregarious Aquarius. Racquet sports, which combine mental strategy and physical conditioning, also attract this sign.

Home and Family

The Aquarius home is a retreat—a place for the Water Bearer to sit back and recharge its batteries. A mix of private and open spaces will fit this sign's needs for both solitude and socializing, and a cool, no-fuss decorating style will suit Aquarius best.

Aquarius parents give their children plenty of autonomy. All important decisions are discussed with the children, and family councils and lively dinner discussions give each child a chance to be heard. Fairness and honesty are the values Aquarians most want to instill in their children.

Children respond enthusiastically to an Aquarius parent because the Water Bearer doesn't talk down to them. This sign appreciates the teenage rebel and admires an independent streak. Aquarius knows how to be a friend to a child and often remains a confidant throughout life.

The Water Bearer won't miss family holidays or reunions. The rest of the time, however, Aquarius is usually too busy to stay in touch.

Careers and Goals

Sympathetic yet able to retain a professional distance, the Water Bearer is particularly effective in helping others organize and develop their talents. Community service and teaching are careers this sign will find meaningful and satisfying.

High technology is also a big draw for Aquarius. The Water Bearer loves gadgets, machinery, and computers and often seeks employment in areas that use these tools to develop systems and ideas that will benefit mankind.

Innovative thinking is another Aquarius talent. This sign comes up with ideas that are way ahead of the pack and often far ahead of their time. Emotion doesn't cloud the Water Bearer's thinking—nor does custom. Aquarius is honest in evaluating its progress: When an idea doesn't work, it is dropped immediately.

Freedom to approach its work in an original way is the key to Aquarius's success in any field.

Pastimes and Play

The Water Bearer is most content in a crowd. Church socials, family reunions, baby showers, wedding receptions—any kind of party will do for gregarious Aquarius.

Many of Aquarius's favorite pastimes involve self-improvement and community action. Esoteric spiritual studies, astrology classes, or meditation retreats—combined with fund-raising, circulating petitions, or working in a soup kitchen—provide the Water Bearer with meaningful off-the-job activities.

Technology excites Aquarius, who loves gadgets, machinery, and computers. So it's not unusual for the Water Bearer to pass up a party to try some new computer software.

Aquarius's favorite sports emphasize speed and strategy, such as tennis and racquetball. Team efforts such as volleyball, soccer, and relay racing also appeal to this sign. If the sport involves a high-tech machine like a sports car or power boat, so much the better.

Love Among the Signs

What is attraction? What is love? Throughout the centuries, science has tried and failed to come up with a satisfying explanation for the mysterious connection between two people.

For the astrologer, the answer is clear. The position of the planets at the time of your birth creates a pattern that influences you throughout your lifetime.

When your pattern meets another person's, the two of you might clash or harmonize.

Why this mysterious connection occurs can be explored only by completing charts for both individuals. But even if the chemistry is there, will it be a happy relationship? Will it last? No one can tell for certain.

Every relationship requires give-and-take, and an awareness of the sun sign relationships can help with this process. The sun sign influences conscious behavior. Does your lover catalog the items in the medicine cabinet? Chances are you have a Virgo on your hands. Do you like to spend your weekends running while your lover wants to play Scrabble? This could be an Aries–Gemini combination.

To discover more about your relationship, find out your lover's sun sign and look under the appropriate combination. You may learn things you had never even suspected.

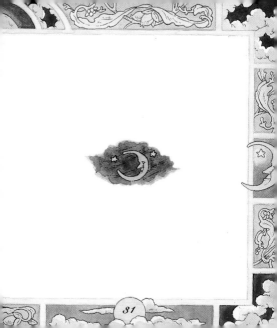

Aquarius with Aries

(March 21–April 20)

The fiery Ram is a doer; the airy Water Bearer is a thinker. This fundamental difference can lead to tension or harmony. Yet since this pairing is one of the most frequently seen astrological combinations, the match often strikes a flame.

Both signs love the thrill of the new. Aquarius is fascinated by the future and by the ideas that will shape it. Aries, a try-anything-once daredevil, prefers the here and now and the physical. The Ram likes to be in the middle of the action—completely absorbed by it. Aquarius prefers a certain amount of detachment. The Water Bearer is a natural spectator, appreciating the game but sitting in the stands to get an overview. For Aries, it's playing the game that counts; for Aquarius, what counts is understanding how the game is played.

In many ways, each sign is just what the other needs. Ideas come easily to Aquarius. Action doesn't. Aries can give Aquarius the push it needs to begin putting its ideas into motion. The Ram is pure energy—flashing toward fleeting targets and often burning itself out without accomplishing anything. Aquarius can help the Ram channel this energy and make it an effective force in the world. The Water Bearer may even convince the self-absorbed Ram to expend some of its wild energy on humanitarian activities.

Both Aquarius and Aries love to talk. Aries talks quickly and spontaneously; Aquarius speaks slowly and logically. This difference in tempo and style can lead to frustration for both if they don't find a way to accommodate each other.

Aquarius's cool detachment is just the sort of sexual challenge the Ram loves. Assertive Aries might take the initiative in lovemaking, but the Water Bearer will soon warm to the chase. As with Scarlett O'Hara (Aries) and Rhett Butler (Aquarius), the sparks will fly between these two signs. And once they ignite, the flames of romance should burn brightly for a long time.

If these two can learn to be patient with each other and continue to be a positive force in each other's lives, they have a good chance at a lasting relationship—one in which they will share new experiences and then move on together.

Aquarius with Taurus

(April 21–May 21)

To Aquarius, there's nothing more delightful than a surprise, just to shake things up a bit. To Taurus, there's nothing more satisfying than things just as they are—the Bull doesn't want its routine shaken. Can these two make it as a couple, or are they on a collision course?

If they can find a common interest, these two signs might work things out. Both must recognize the major differences in their views of the world. To Aquarius, an air sign, the "real world" is the world of the mind. Imagination, innovation, and principle stir the soul of Aquarius. Earth sign Taurus lives in the physical world. The Bull doesn't want to have its soul stirred, it wants security and creature comforts. Food in the cupboard and a well-stocked video library are more important to Taurus than politics, technology, the future of the human race, or anything else that gets the Water Bearer so worked up.

Aquarius is a visionary who sees the future as a golden dream; Taurus is a realist who saves its money to make its dreams come true.

Both the Bull and the Water Bearer are terribly stubborn—a characteristic that must be overcome if they are to be of any good to each other. Taurus could teach Aquarius to be more practical, and Aquarius could help the Bull become more flexible.

Aquarius and Taurus are usually very even tempered. But watch out when they get angry: Their rages can be devastating. The Water Bearer's rage is a powerful outpouring of long-suppressed emotion. The Bull's rage is a destructive rush of energy. Aquarius is usually embarrassed by its outburst, while Taurus never is.

Sexual communication could prove

difficult for this couple. Taurus is possessive and needs plenty of cuddling and other physical demonstrations of affection. Aquarius has a detached, experimental approach to sex and balks at any sign of possessiveness. The Water Bearer's wide range of friends is sure to provoke the Bull's jealousy, and with Aquarius constantly on the go, Taurus might feel neglected and seek fulfillment elsewhere.

A genuine interest in each other's world will be needed to keep this couple together.

Aquarius with Gemini
(May 22–June 21)

When Gemini meets Aquarius, there's no middle ground: It's either love or hate.

Unlike water signs, who experience the world emotionally, and earth signs, who experience the world sensually, air signs Gemini and Aquarius experience the world intellectually.

Gemini and Aquarius may be attracted to each other at first because they believe they are both operating on the same wavelength. However, as their relationship progresses they may discover this isn't the case.

Gemini has a quick mind, gathers information from many sources, and knows a little bit about a lot of things. This sign is far more interested in its immediate surroundings and social life than in the larger issues that concern Aquarius.

The Water Bearer is always seeking the one eternal truth that links everything. However, Gemini doesn't believe in absolute truth. To Gemini, truth is relative and what is true for one person may not be true for another.

These fundamentally different perspectives could lead to many misunderstandings between these two. To avoid conflict, Aquarius must loosen up, learn to relax its rigid standards, and acknowledge that there are many ways to view the world. In turn, Gemini must find a way to focus and direct its energies toward achieving more far-reaching goals.

Communication is this couple's strong point. They should be able to talk out their differences easily. They will find each other's conversation more engaging and entertaining than going to the movies or watching television. An active social life and a wide circle of friends and acquaintances will be shared

42

by these two—providing them with endless topics of conversation.

Sexually, this couple should be harmonious, giving each other pleasure with delightful surprises and diverse techniques. Neither of them will burden their lovemaking with heavy emotions.

With very little effort, the Water Bearer and Gemini can find common ground and share a mentally stimulating, playful, and romantic relationship.

Aquarius with Cancer
(June 22–July 23)

Aquarius and Cancer are most happy when they are helping others. But they go about it in quite different ways. Aquarius prefers interacting with large groups; Cancer excels at one-on-one intimacy. The Water Bearer approaches situations and people with cool detachment, while the Crab takes everything and everyone personally.

Cancer is fascinated by the way Aquarius can be so concerned for humanity and yet remain so personally distant. For the highly sensitive Crab, who reacts to the slightest emotional nuance, such dispassion is remarkable.

The Crab draws strength from security, home, and loved ones. But the Water Bearer needs a steady stream of new experiences and a stimulating social life to feel fulfilled.

The Crab will make sure the Water Bearer eats right, sleeps enough, and keeps track of the car keys. Though after a while, this kind of hovering attention could drive Aquarius right up the wall. The Water Bearer needs freedom, and

Cancer must be willing to let go a bit if this relationship is going to work.

Neither sign is comfortable living in the present. Aquarius dreams of the future; Cancer pines for the past. Each must learn to appreciate its partner's perspective to avoid conflict.

Adopting each other's good qualities is one way to make this relationship thrive. For example, in order to deal with Aquarius's blunt honesty, Cancer must learn to be more direct and not nurse hurt feelings. And to live harmoniously with the tender-hearted Crab, Aquarius must strive to be more emotionally sensitive.

Money should cause no problems between these two. The Water Bearer cares little about it, and the Crab is a terrific money manager.

Sexually this couple will get along well provided they balance Aquarius's love for novelty with Cancer's need for tenderness.

As illustrated by former president Ronald Reagan (Aquarius) and his wife, Nancy (Cancer), this pairing can be a huge success. Though often considered remote by others, President Reagan made his adoring wife feel special. In turn, she protected and supported him.

Aquarius with Leo
(July 24–August 23)

W hen the natural democrat meets the natural monarch, the combination can be explosive.

These two signs, opposite each other in the zodiac, are attracted by qualities they admire and may secretly envy. Leo makes friends easily. The Lion is a fire sign, with a natural warmth that envelops everyone it meets. Aquarius, a cerebral air sign, could benefit from Leo's social graces, especially in one-on-one situations where the Water Bearer finds it difficult to communicate.

The valor of idealistic Aquarius, championing unpopular causes, greatly impresses the Lion. Both Aquarius and Leo work for the underdog—Leo giving hands-on help to those in need and Aquarius recruiting others to lend a hand.

Negotiating an equal partnership could be tricky. Leo's natural charisma makes it the center of any gathering and often results in a leadership role for the Lion. But Aquarius doesn't believe in leaders. Why should one person's opinion be given more weight than another's? Dividing the turf may be the best solution for this pair.

Aquarius and Leo both love busy social and professional lives but think of themselves as somewhat above it all. Aquarius is an observer rather than a participant; Leo is a leader rather than a follower. Yet the Lion is basically traditional and cares deeply about what other people think. The unconventional Water Bearer may have to tone down its opinions (publicly, at least) if it is to keep the Lion happy.

Egalitarian Aquarius would rather knock a monarch off its throne than pay it homage. However, Leo craves applause, loud and clear, and will get it one way or another. Aquarius had better be generous with praise if it wants to tame the Lion.

Sexual compatibility depends on whether the Water Bearer is willing to stroke the Lion's ego continually. If given the royal treatment, Leo will give a star performance. But if this sign isn't treated like royalty, it may roam until it finds a more devoted subject.

If Aquarius is willing to make Leo the center of its universe, these two can have a warm and lasting relationship.

Aquarius with Virgo

(August 24–September 23)

A quarius is an idealistic air sign; Virgo is a practical earth sign. The Water Bearer deals in generalities; the Virgin deals in specifics. Can these two get along?

If they can reconcile their differences, these two will be assets to each other. Virgo can bring Aquarius down to earth and help it deal with the practical realities of life. Aquarius can introduce the Virgin to a broad range of experiences and give it a cause to work for.

However, it will take more than a casual meeting to light a spark between these two. Both may hesitate to make the first move since they will be busy sizing each other up. Once they get to know each other, though, they will be impressed by each other's natural intelligence.

Aquarius is concerned with the large issues and the moral ramifications of any action. Virgo is less concerned with right or wrong and more concerned with what's practical—what works and what doesn't. For example, if this couple is deciding to buy a car, Aquarius may choose the model that gets the best mileage in order to conserve Earth's natural resources; Virgo may choose the same car but only because it saves them money or is big enough for the dog.

Virgo's facility with details could be a boon to the Water Bearer. Balancing the budget, figuring out how to work that new appliance, keeping track of appointments—these are all things the detail-oriented Virgo does effortlessly. The dangers here are that Virgo may feel it is forever picking up loose ends, and the Water Bearer may begin to chafe under Virgo's exacting perfectionism.

As business partners, these two will make a good team. As lovers, it will be more difficult. Neither sign is particularly passionate, and the relationship may suffer from lack of energy. In addition, both signs are shy about commitment. Even when they are in love (or especially when they are), Aquarius and Virgo hesitate to take the plunge.

A good, basic friendship might give this pair time to adjust to each other's needs and styles. And who knows: Once they have a meeting of the minds, they might discover the way to each other's heart.

57

Aquarius with Libra
(September 24–October 23)

Poised, graceful, and charming—
nearly everyone is attracted to
Libra. But to the Water Bearer,
this sign is positively irresistible. Aquarius will be glad to know the feeling is
mutual.

Both are sociable air signs. Aquarius
prefers large groups, while Libra enjoys
more intimate gatherings. Most likely
these two will meet at a party or the

workplace, where they will be off to the side keeping an eye on the action.

Because Libra is one of the most indecisive signs of the zodiac, this couple could have a hard time working things out. Libra compulsively sees all sides of an issue and, in order to avoid conflict, may avoid dealing with serious problems altogether. However, Aquarius is stimulated by lively discussions. If the Water Bearer can get Libra to talk things out, this couple may find they are in agreement on the truly important issues, and minor differences, once aired, will be easily resolved.

Since Aquarius often has a freewheeling and erratic lifestyle, compromise may be required to accommodate Libra's need for a balanced life. Small things, like sharing meals and sleeping at regular hours, are important to Libra.

Conflict can also arise over Libra's need to be part of a couple (Libra is often called the "marriage" sign) versus Aquarius's need to be free. These two must find a way to give each other enough space and at the same time be true partners who are available when needed.

Libra and Aquarius are intellectual dreamers who find planning a project easy and fun and doing a project hard and dull. They need help to make their dreams a reality.

Lovemaking, rather than sex for its own sake, is a form of communication for this couple. Libra brings out the buried romantic side of Aquarius, and the Water Bearer's originality in the bedroom is liberating for Libra.

With the natural harmony and understanding between these two signs, Aquarius may have found the ideal combination of friend and lover.

N either Aquarius nor Scorpio is as it seems on the surface. Under its gregarious exterior, Aquarius hides the soul of a loner. Under its cool veneer, Scorpio hides a well of feelings.

Even though Scorpio is a deeply emotional water sign, it conceals its feelings rather than expose itself to possible pain. The sign of the Scorpion shields itself by manipulating others and getting what it wants from them without their knowing. Scorpio will have to be much more aboveboard with Aquarius, who dislikes scheming of any kind.

Scorpio may admire the Water Bearer's altruism, but it won't appreciate Aquarius's neglectful attitude toward personal relationships. To Aquarius, putting too much energy into a relationship is like saying your private desires are more important than the needs of all the impoverished people on the planet.

At first, Aquarius may find Scorpio's emotional intensity attractive. But this sign's all-or-nothing approach can push the independent Aquarius out the door fast, once the initial infatuation is over. And Scorpio won't appreciate the Water Bearer's full calendar unless there are a lot of shared activities penciled in.

Compromise is difficult for these two signs because both are stubborn and neither likes to give in. Calm discussion of financial and household responsibilities could deflect conflicts—particularly when thrifty Scorpio comes up against spend-thrift Water Bearer. On the positive side, they will admire each other's mental sharpness. The Water Bearer is a great analyzer, and the Scorpion is a terrific detective. These two won't have many secrets from each other.

Sexually, these two will take off—at

first. The inventive Aquarius will please and excite the adventurous Scorpio. However, Scorpio's jealousy may put a damper on the freewheeling Water Bearer's style, and resentment can arise when Aquarius feels compelled to have an explanation for every absence.

This is a very challenging pair. If fate brings this couple together, both will have to set aside their fixed ideas and work hard to understand and accommodate each other.

Aquarius with Sagittarius
(November 23–December 21)

When a passionate fire sign and an electric air sign get together, sparks are sure to fly.

A natural respect exists between Aquarius and Sagittarius. They do not always agree, but they understand each other on a deep level. These two have similar principles, and because they agree on the most important issues, they can disagree about everything else. In fact, verbal sparring is one of the ways these two make love. They secretly relish every parry and thrust of their verbal duels.

Sagittarius is one of the few signs that can bring out the fun and warmth in the normally reserved and detached Aquarius. The sign of the Archer has a zest for living and, like Aquarius, a hunger for new experiences. However, distant goals are hard for Sagittarius to keep in focus, so the Water Bearer's guidance in this area is a great asset to the Archer.

Sagittarius often offends people by speaking the brutal, uncensored truth. The Archer has the ability to recognize falsehoods and cut through meaningless chatter. Aquarius appreciates the Archer's honesty—the Water Bearer never minds hearing the truth, even when it's unpleasant.

This couple enjoys a busy life. Sagittarius likes to be where the action is, while Aquarius enjoys reaching out to as many kinds of people as possible. These two are sure to be involved together in community affairs.

Many of their mutual interests will involve helping others. Abused children, disaster victims, endangered species— both of these signs are truly concerned about such issues. The Water Bearer will work tirelessly organizing others and seeking solutions to these problems; the

Archer is more likely to help by donating money and material goods.

Sagittarius's passion and Aquarius's originality can make for fireworks in the bedroom. Both signs are erotic adventurers who will bring laughter and fun to lovemaking.

A relationship with Sagittarius could be the most rewarding one possible for Aquarius. These signs understand each other, feel free to be themselves together, and respect one another's individuality—all necessary components for a lasting relationship.

Aquarius with Capricorn

(December 22–January 20)

These two signs make good neighbors in the zodiac and, with work, can become successful partners as well. Tradition-minded Capricorn is drawn to Aquarius because it wants to be put in touch with "what's happening." The Water Bearer senses a kinship with this sign and recognizes many aspects of itself in the Goat. Though they express themselves differently, both are hard-working, ambitious, and driven. However, en route to success, Aquarius will always put the common good above personal gain; Capricorn won't. The Goat may form alliances, but its primary concern will always be its own advancement.

One challenge to this relationship will come when the Goat's aristocratic attitude clashes with the Water Bearer's democratic stance. Prestige and status symbols, so important to Capricorn, mean little in the Water Bearer's world, where all people are equal. Ironically, Aquarius often receives the honor and recognition so coveted by Capricorn.

Another significant difference between these two is their attitudes toward change. The Goat prefers to stick with what has worked in the past. Aquarius embraces the future and welcomes change. In a marriage this could mean a great deal of compromise as the Goat learns to accommodate the Water Bearer's busy schedule and Aquarius acknowledges the Goat's desire for a traditional home structure.

Capricorn can get Aquarius organized and set the Water Bearer's ideas into motion. The Goat has the ability to weed out the Water Bearer's pie-in-the-sky dreams from those that can be realized. A Capricorn can never be persuaded to do something that won't get results, no matter how noble the idea.

Capricorn finds Aquarius's openness appealing. Yet the Goat is secretive, which may cause distress to Aquarius. The Water Bearer is most comfortable when all the cards are on the table. But the Goat never shows its hand.

Sexually, this can be a rather cool combination, with both signs on different wavelengths. However, if friendship and trust are established mutual affection could lead to a more satisfying and intimate relationship—in bed and out.

Aquarius with Aquarius

(January 21–February 19)

W ho can understand the complex, contradictory Aquarius better than another Aquarius? Sharing the same needs and drives gives partners of the same sign an unspoken understanding. This is especially comforting to Aquarius, who always feels a little different from the rest of humanity and is often misunderstood, even by close friends.

Since these partners do not play by ordinary rules, they will have to invent their relationship as they go along. They may begin as casual friends with no inkling of a romantic future. But if they recognize how much they have in common and allow their feelings to develop, love may blossom.

These two will insist on an equal partnership, though they may interpret equality in a highly original way. The female breadwinner and male homemaker is only one example of the role reversals common with this pair.

Even though Aquarius loves being in a group of people, it also needs plenty of time to itself. If the Water Bearer doesn't call for a week, it's simply because it needs some solitude. Both partners will understand this need for time alone, so neither will feel neglected if the phone doesn't ring or one partner takes off for a while. After all, they each have plenty of friends and activities to keep themselves occupied.

Aquarius judges people by the company they keep. Sharing friends and interests will be an important part of this match. In fact, too many separate interests could be disruptive.

There are always ups and downs in a double Aquarius relationship. These signs should expect the unexpected—a life full of surprises. The eccentric

Aquarius nature ensures that this partnership will never settle into something bland and routine. There will always be some new idea to explore or problem to solve.

Sexually, nothing shocks this pair, so their lovemaking will be liberated and full of erotic adventures. The only problem will be taking time from their busy schedules to be alone together.

This couple admires each other's virtues, since they are shared. If they can forgive each other's flaws, also shared, they might become true soul mates.

Aquarius with Pisces
(February 20–March 20)

A quarius can usually figure people out pretty easily—but that's not the case with Pisces. This water sign, like its symbol the Fish, is slippery and slides out of any category that Aquarius tries to put it into.

Emotionally, these two are on different wavelengths. Like other air signs, Aquarius would rather not deal with messy feelings. The highly intuitive

Fish, who lives in a world of dreams and emotions, has little need for logic. Pisces is quiet because the things that matter to it are the things that cannot be put into words.

The sensitive Fish absorbs every emotional shift in its environment and changes constantly in reaction to it. Aquarius, on the other hand, is a steady, detached observer who analyzes everything from a safe distance. And Pisces' vagueness with the truth can be very frustrating for Aquarius. But Pisces can't help it: To the Fish, nothing is cut and dried—everything is relative.

Managing money will be a challenge for these two nonmaterialistic signs.

Both need a steady income to support their dreams and achieve their goals; however, neither likes to budget or save. It might be best for them to bring in a more earthbound sign to handle money matters.

Pisces' imagination will blend well with Aquarius's forward vision to make this a very creative relationship. This creativity will not be expressed in the usual channels; rather, it will be there in the way they deal with people. Come-as-you-are parties, unexpected gifts, whimsical games—spontaneity reigns in this couple's social life. They delight in finding original ways to show their affection to their friends and loved ones.

As a mutable sign, Pisces will adapt to Aquarius's habits, though this doesn't mean all will be smooth sailing. Pisces is a very emotional and empathetic sign. But Aquarius isn't deeply affected by emotions.

In the bedroom, Aquarius must be particularly sensitive since Pisces rarely states its needs directly. However, if the Water Bearer can read the Fish's subtle, indirect signals, this pair can enjoy a satisfying sex life. And a good relationship, too.

The text of this book was set in
Bembo and the display in Caslon Open Face
by Crane Typesetting Service, Inc.,
West Barnstable, Massachusetts.

Book design and illustrations by
JUDITH A. STAGNITTO